PHOTO FUN PICTURE PUZZLES

PEOPLE

THUNDER BAY
P·R·E·S·S
San Diego, California

Thunder Bay Press
An imprint of the Baker & Taylor Publishing Group
10350 Barnes Canyon Road, San Diego, CA 92121
www.thunderbaybooks.com

Copyright © Thunder Bay, 2011

Design, layout, and photo manipulation by
quadrum▪
www.quadrumltd.com

ISBN-13: 978-1-60701-224-3
ISBN-10: 1-60710-224-2

Printed in India.

Contents

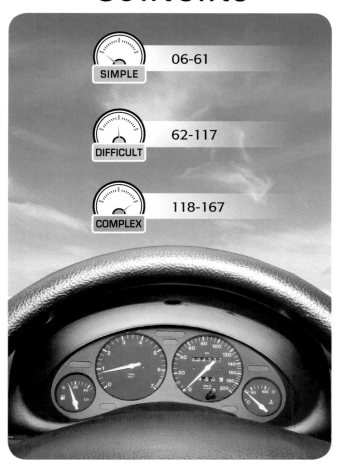

SIMPLE 06-61

DIFFICULT 62-117

COMPLEX 118-167

SPOT THE USAGE

Types of puzzles

This book has three types of puzzles with one, two, or eight pictures on every page. Each puzzle may have five to ten differences, or an odd image that you have to spot.

ONE PICTURE PER PAGE

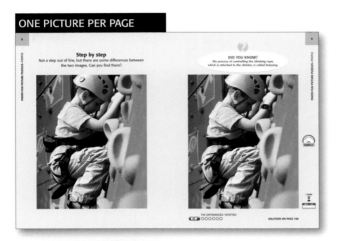

Compare the pictures on two opposite pages and spot the differences between them.

TWO PICTURES PER PAGE

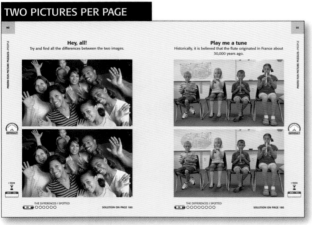

Compare two pictures on the same page and spot the differences between them.

EIGHT PICTURES PER PAGE

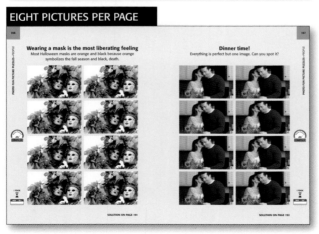

Look at all eight pictures on the same page and spot the odd one out.

Symbols used

1

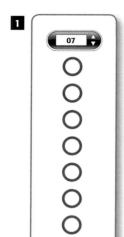

Tick off circle for every difference you find.

2

DID YOU KNOW?
Studies have proved that happy people live longer, make more money, and receive better job reviews.

Included is a "Did You Know" fact to keep you interested as you go about spotting the differences!

3

SOLUTIONS ON PAGE 100

Help is close at hand. Just turn to the correct page to see the answers.

4

Record the time you take to find all the differences.

Difficulty meters

The sections are color coded to be in line with the difficulty meter. This is helpful in identifying the level of complexity of each puzzle. See how far you can push yourself!

SIMPLE

DIFFICULT

COMPLEX

Step by step

Not a step out of line, but there are some differences between the two images. Can you find them?

DID YOU KNOW?
*The process of controlling the climbing rope,
which is attached to the climber, is called belaying.*

SIMPLE

I TOOK

MIN : SEC

THE DIFFERENCES I SPOTTED

06

SOLUTION ON PAGE 168

Ying and yang

Restore the balance by finding all the differences between the images.

SIMPLE

I TOOK

MIN : SEC

THE DIFFERENCES I SPOTTED

06 ○○○○○○

SOLUTION ON PAGE 168

Catch of the day!

"Noodling" is when one catches the catfish with their bare hands.
Do you think you can catch all the differences between the two images?

SIMPLE

I TOOK

MIN : SEC

THE DIFFERENCES I SPOTTED

08

SOLUTION ON PAGE 168

Row, row, row your boat
Can you find all the differences between these two images?

SIMPLE

I TOOK

MIN : SEC

THE DIFFERENCES I SPOTTED

06 ○○○○○○

SOLUTION ON PAGE 168

You take my breath away

To bring good fortune, Buddhist prayer flags are strung between mountains all over Ladakh and other parts of the Himalayas.

SIMPLE

I TOOK

MIN : SEC

THE DIFFERENCES I SPOTTED

08 ○○○○○○○○

SOLUTION ON PAGE 168

United in peace

"A smile is the beginning of peace." – Anonymous

SIMPLE

I TOOK

MIN : SEC

THE DIFFERENCES I SPOTTED

06 ○○○○○○

SOLUTION ON PAGE 168

A boxer's handshake

American boxer Riddick Bowe is the only fighter to hold all four world title belts—IBF, WBA, WBC, and WBO.

SIMPLE

I TOOK

MIN : SEC

THE DIFFERENCES I SPOTTED

SOLUTION ON PAGE 169

Wheeeeeeeee!
The Native American term for snow sled is *toboggan.*

SIMPLE

I TOOK

MIN : SEC

THE DIFFERENCES I SPOTTED

06 ⬍ ○○○○○○

SOLUTION ON PAGE 169

Something old, something new

"Whatever souls are made of, his and mine are the same."
– Emily Bronte

SIMPLE

I TOOK

MIN : SEC

THE DIFFERENCES I SPOTTED

09 ○○○○○○○○○

SOLUTION ON PAGE 169

Pretty day, pretty me

On this perfect day, try and locate the one image that is odd.

SIMPLE

I TOOK

MIN : SEC

SOLUTION ON PAGE 169

Let's go diving!

Don't hold your breath, try and find the odd one out.

SIMPLE

I TOOK

MIN : SEC

SOLUTION ON PAGE 169

Let's dance all night!
Before the concert ends, try and spot the odd image.

SIMPLE

I TOOK

MIN : SEC

SOLUTION ON PAGE 169

Dancing to my own beat
The Sun Dance is a religious ceremony performed by several Native American communities and tribes such as the Arapaho and Ute.

SIMPLE

I TOOK

MIN : SEC

SOLUTION ON PAGE 170

Winter wonderland

Even though these two images look alike,
there are eight differences. Can you spot them?

DID YOU KNOW?
Tom Sims modified the skateboard and made the first snowboard in 1963.

SIMPLE

I TOOK

MIN : SEC

THE DIFFERENCES I SPOTTED

08 ○○○○○○○○

SOLUTION ON PAGE 170

Questioning authority

You may be able to answer their questions, by spotting all the differences between the two images.

SIMPLE

I TOOK

MIN : SEC

THE DIFFERENCES I SPOTTED

06 ⬍ ○○○○○○

SOLUTION ON PAGE 170

Afloat with happiness

Try and find all the differences between these two family portraits.

SIMPLE

I TOOK

MIN : SEC

THE DIFFERENCES I SPOTTED

07 ○○○○○○○

SOLUTION ON PAGE 170

With you all the way

"Other things may change us, but we start and end with family."
– Anthony Brandt

SIMPLE

I TOOK

MIN : SEC

THE DIFFERENCES I SPOTTED

07 ○○○○○○○

SOLUTION ON PAGE 170

Male bonding at its best
"It is not flesh and blood but the heart, which makes us fathers and sons." – Johann Schiller

SIMPLE

I TOOK

MIN : SEC

THE DIFFERENCES I SPOTTED

08 ○○○○○○○○

SOLUTION ON PAGE 170

Well done, mate!
Try and find all the differences between the two images.

SIMPLE

I TOOK

MIN : SEC

THE DIFFERENCES I SPOTTED

07 ○○○○○○○

SOLUTION ON PAGE 171

Human pentagon in the heavens

Before this daring bunch opens their parachutes, try and find all the differences between the two images.

SIMPLE

I TOOK

MIN : SEC

THE DIFFERENCES I SPOTTED

07 ○○○○○○○

SOLUTION ON PAGE 171

The baby munch bunch

Without getting too distracted by all the cuteness, try and locate all the differences between the images.

SIMPLE

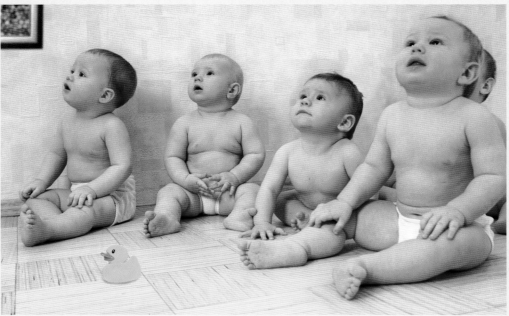

I TOOK

MIN : SEC

THE DIFFERENCES I SPOTTED

05 ○○○○○

SOLUTION ON PAGE 171

My world, my friends

"A friend is one who knows you and loves you just the same."
– Elbert Hubbard

SIMPLE

I TOOK

MIN : SEC

THE DIFFERENCES I SPOTTED

08 ○○○○○○○○

SOLUTION ON PAGE 171

One step at a time

Established in 1872, Yellowstone National Park is America's first national park.

SIMPLE

I TOOK

MIN : SEC

SOLUTION ON PAGE 171

Cruising at our own pace

Can you find the odd image before these kayakers stop to set up camp?

SIMPLE

I TOOK

MIN : SEC

SOLUTION ON PAGE 171

Color in my step. Color in my life.

As dazzling as her outfit is, can you locate the odd image?

SIMPLE

I TOOK

MIN : SEC

SOLUTION ON PAGE 172

Geronimo!

Spot the odd image.

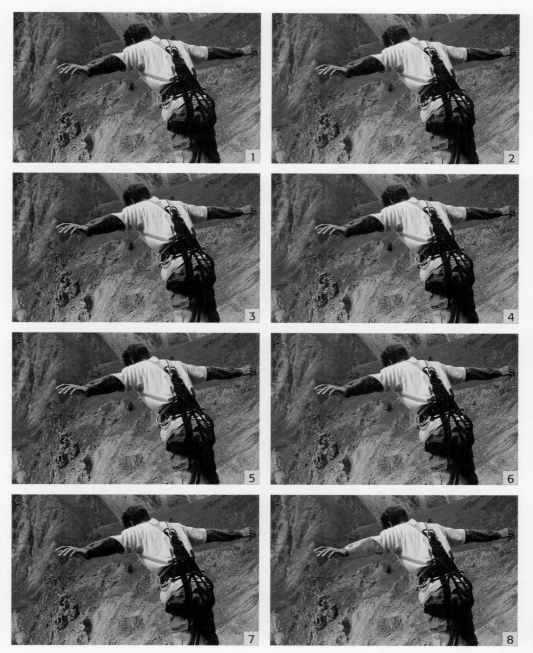

SIMPLE

I TOOK

MIN : SEC

SOLUTION ON PAGE 172

Travel fun!

"Celebrate the happiness that friends are always giving, make every day a holiday and celebrate just living!" – Amanda Bradley

DID YOU KNOW?
Greece's mainland, as well as the quaint islands that surround it, have many historical sites that one feels like revisiting again and again.

SIMPLE

I TOOK

MIN : SEC

THE DIFFERENCES I SPOTTED

SOLUTION ON PAGE 172

Time for a sundown party!
Ibiza in Spain and Mykonos in Greece are islands that are popular for their crazy beach parties.

SIMPLE

I TOOK

MIN : SEC

THE DIFFERENCES I SPOTTED

06 ○○○○○○

SOLUTION ON PAGE 172

A trek to paradise

The High Tatras, a mountain range in Slovakia bordering Poland, is very famous for its treks.

SIMPLE

I TOOK

MIN : SEC

THE DIFFERENCES I SPOTTED

SOLUTION ON PAGE 172

Nothing like some good old sibling rivalry

Before the kids hit the water, see if you can find all the differences between the two images.

SIMPLE

I TOOK

MIN : SEC

THE DIFFERENCES I SPOTTED

06 ○○○○○○

SOLUTION ON PAGE 172

Volleyed out

Todd Rogers, an Olympic gold medalist, along with partner
Phil Dalhausser, make the best U.S. men's beach volleyball duo.

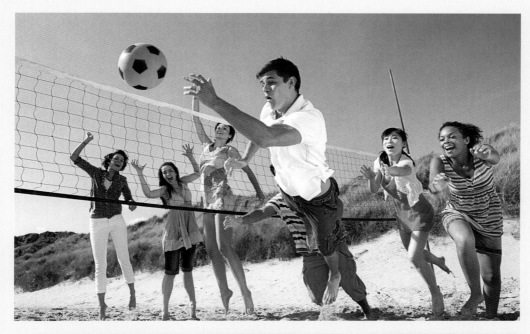

SIMPLE

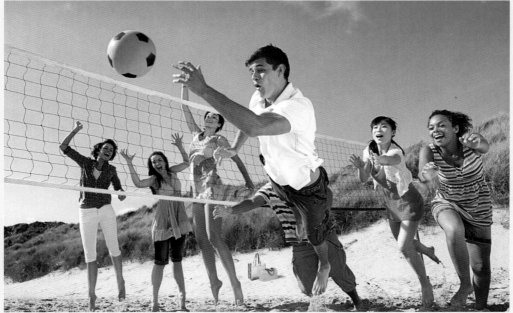

I TOOK

MIN : SEC

THE DIFFERENCES I SPOTTED

07 ○○○○○○○

SOLUTION ON PAGE 173

No snow angel here
One is never too old for games, especially snowball fights.
Try and spot all the differences as quickly as possible.

SIMPLE

I TOOK

MIN : SEC

THE DIFFERENCES I SPOTTED

08 ○○○○○○○○

SOLUTION ON PAGE 173

Hop, skip, jump, let's shop!
The Mall of America opened in 1992 in Bloomington, Minnesota. It is the largest mall in the United States.

SIMPLE

I TOOK

MIN : SEC

THE DIFFERENCES I SPOTTED

SOLUTION ON PAGE 173

Pink, yellow, or green?
Can you spot the odd image?

SIMPLE

I TOOK

MIN : SEC

SOLUTION ON PAGE 173

My precious bundle of mischief

Anna Jarvis founded Mother's Day on May 10, 1908, and it was President Woodrow Wilson who made it a national holiday.

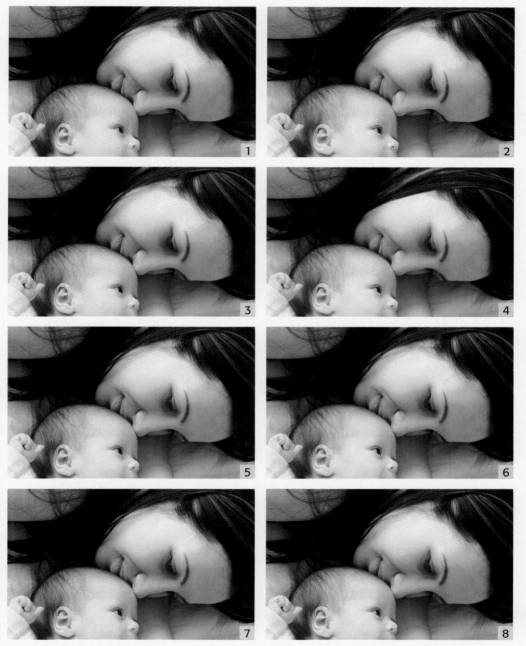

SIMPLE

I TOOK

MIN : SEC

SOLUTION ON PAGE 173

Shape up!
It's a weighing issue. Can you spot the odd image?

SIMPLE

I TOOK

MIN : SEC

SOLUTION ON PAGE 173

Discovery unbound

There are plenty of discoveries but only one odd image.
Can you find it?

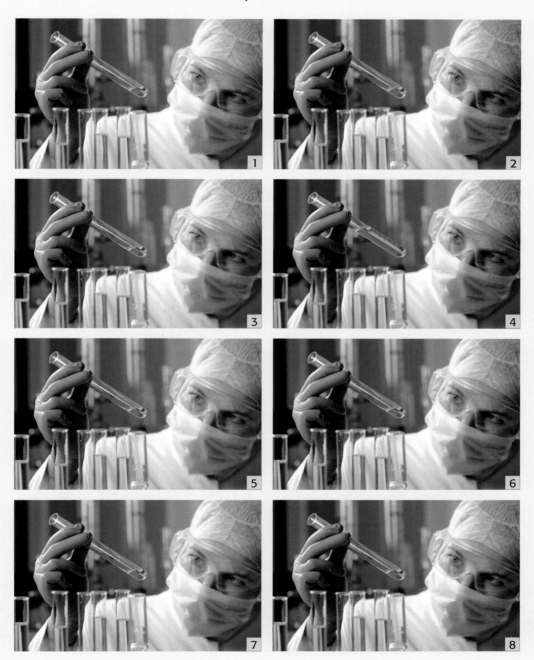

SIMPLE

I TOOK

MIN : SEC

SOLUTION ON PAGE 174

Up and away!

"Imagination is the highest kite one can fly." – Lauren Bacall

DID YOU KNOW?
In 1752, Benjamin Franklin flew a kite in a thunderstorm that resulted in him proving that lightning is a natural phenomenon and not a supernatural one.

SIMPLE

I TOOK

MIN : SEC

THE DIFFERENCES I SPOTTED

08 ○○○○○○○○

SOLUTION ON PAGE 174

Sticky statistics

Systematically or otherwise, try and find all the differences between the two images.

SIMPLE

I TOOK

MIN : SEC

THE DIFFERENCES I SPOTTED

07

SOLUTION ON PAGE 174

It's always fun with mom

While the little boy entertains his mom and little sister, try and spot all the differences between the two images.

SIMPLE

I TOOK

MIN : SEC

THE DIFFERENCES I SPOTTED

06 ○○○○○○

SOLUTION ON PAGE 174

Hats of fun

The first rimmed hat was called the *Phrygian* cap, worn by freed Greek and Roman slaves in the early half of the sixteenth century.

SIMPLE

I TOOK

MIN : SEC

THE DIFFERENCES I SPOTTED

05 ○○○○○   SOLUTION ON PAGE 174

Engineering the future

Eleven American buildings have held the title of "tallest building in the world." Eight were in New York City and seven in Chicago.

SIMPLE

I TOOK

MIN : SEC

THE DIFFERENCES I SPOTTED

08 ⬍ ○○○○○○○○

SOLUTION ON PAGE 174

A walk in the park

Solving this puzzle may not be as easy as a walk in the park but it will surely be as fun.

SIMPLE

I TOOK

MIN : SEC

THE DIFFERENCES I SPOTTED

08 ○○○○○○○○

SOLUTION ON PAGE 175

For the fun of the game

"Some people think football is a matter of life and death.
I assure you, it's much more serious than that." – Bill Shankly

SIMPLE

I TOOK

MIN : SEC

THE DIFFERENCES I SPOTTED

09 ○○○○○○○○○

SOLUTION ON PAGE 175

Riot Police
Try and locate all the differences between the two images?

SIMPLE

I TOOK

MIN : SEC

THE DIFFERENCES I SPOTTED

09 ○○○○○○○○○

SOLUTION ON PAGE 175

New kids on the block

To date, Britain's most successful boy band has been *Take That*.

SIMPLE

I TOOK

MIN : SEC

THE DIFFERENCES I SPOTTED

06 ○○○○○○

SOLUTION ON PAGE 175

Best friends forever

The girls are enjoying a lovely evening. You can too while solving this fun puzzle!

SIMPLE

I TOOK

MIN : SEC

THE DIFFERENCES I SPOTTED

06 ○○○○○○

SOLUTION ON PAGE 175

Young love

In German, Valentine's Day is called *Valentinstag*.

SIMPLE

I TOOK

MIN : SEC

THE DIFFERENCES I SPOTTED

05 ○○○○○

SOLUTION ON PAGE 175

Love, the ingredient needed for that perfect meal

"There is only one happiness in life—to love and to be loved."
— George Sand

SIMPLE

I TOOK

MIN : SEC

THE DIFFERENCES I SPOTTED

07 ○○○○○○○

SOLUTION ON PAGE 176

The hills are alive with the sound of music
The alphorn, traditionally used by herdsmen in the 1800s,
is the national musical instrument of Switzerland.

SIMPLE

I TOOK

MIN : SEC

THE DIFFERENCES I SPOTTED

SOLUTION ON PAGE 176

DIFFICULT

Spool me silly

"There is no time for cut-and-dried monotony. There is time for work. And time for love. That leaves no other time." – Coco Chanel

DID YOU KNOW?
The perfume Chanel No. 5 was the first to be a blend of a variety of floral scents.

DIFFICULT

I TOOK

MIN : SEC

THE DIFFERENCES I SPOTTED

10 ◯◯◯◯◯◯◯◯◯◯

SOLUTION ON PAGE 176

Giddy up!

The concept of "cowboys" originated in Spain. They brought this method of cattle ranching to America in the sixteenth century.

DIFFICULT

I TOOK

MIN : SEC

THE DIFFERENCES I SPOTTED

07

SOLUTION ON PAGE 176

Summer fun
Tulum, Playa del Carmen, Huatulco, and Acapulco are some of the top beaches of Mexico.

DIFFICULT

I TOOK

MIN : SEC

THE DIFFERENCES I SPOTTED

06

SOLUTION ON PAGE 176

I'm always ready for Mardi Gras

The Venetian mask that covers the entire face was traditionally
worn as a piece of art and is called the *bauta*.

DIFFICULT

I TOOK

MIN : SEC

THE DIFFERENCES I SPOTTED

08 ○○○○○○○○

SOLUTION ON PAGE 176

Building a better tomorrow
Architect of the Year Awards is held annually in November.
The winner of 2009 was Richard Feilden.

DIFFICULT

I TOOK

MIN : SEC

THE DIFFERENCES I SPOTTED

SOLUTION ON PAGE 177

Deep blue sea

See how long you take to discover all the differences
between these two pictures.

DIFFICULT

I TOOK

MIN : SEC

THE DIFFERENCES I SPOTTED

SOLUTION ON PAGE 177

Hi Ya!

Dekimasu, pronounced, "day-kee-mahss" means
"I can do it" in Japanese.

I TOOK

MIN : SEC

THE DIFFERENCES I SPOTTED

08 ○○○○○○○○

SOLUTION ON PAGE 177

Laughter among friends
Can you figure out all the differences between the two images?

DIFFICULT

I TOOK

MIN : SEC

THE DIFFERENCES I SPOTTED

08 ○○○○○○○○

SOLUTION ON PAGE 177

Now, let's go there

While these hikers decide which mountain to conquer next,
see if you can find all the differences between the two images.

DIFFICULT

I TOOK

MIN : SEC

THE DIFFERENCES I SPOTTED

06 ◇ ○○○○○○

SOLUTION ON PAGE 177

Nowhere to go but up!

"The best climber in the world is the one who's having the most fun." – Alex Lowe

1

2

3

4

5

6

7

8

DIFFICULT

I TOOK

MIN : SEC

SOLUTION ON PAGE 177

Every player needs a strategy

Except for America, almost every country in the world calls soccer "football."

DIFFICULT

I TOOK

MIN : SEC

SOLUTION ON PAGE 178

Tranquility personified

With a calm mind, try and spot all the differences between these two beautiul images.

DID YOU KNOW?
The Mughal emperor Aurangzeb destroyed the original Golden Temple and built a mosque in its place.

DIFFICULT

I TOOK

MIN : SEC

THE DIFFERENCES I SPOTTED

10 ○○○○○○○○○○

SOLUTION ON PAGE 178

Magnificent wastelands

In Arabic the term "caravan" refers to the pilgrims and merchants
that crossed the Sahara Desert

DIFFICULT

I TOOK

MIN : SEC

THE DIFFERENCES I SPOTTED

07 ○○○○○○○

SOLUTION ON PAGE 178

Medical marvels
Can you find all the differences between the two images?

DIFFICULT

I TOOK

MIN : SEC

THE DIFFERENCES I SPOTTED

06 ○○○○○○

SOLUTION ON PAGE 178

Walking the holy path

Vesaka, informally known as Buddha's birthday, is an annual holiday celebrated by Buddhists all around the world.

DIFFICULT

I TOOK

MIN : SEC

THE DIFFERENCES I SPOTTED

08 ○○○○○○○○

SOLUTION ON PAGE 178

Bring it on, let's race!
As quickly as you can, try and find all the differences between the images.

DIFFICULT

I TOOK

MIN : SEC

THE DIFFERENCES I SPOTTED

06 ○○○○○○

SOLUTION ON PAGE 178

Office space

Spot all the differences between the images.

DIFFICULT

I TOOK

MIN : SEC

THE DIFFERENCES I SPOTTED

09 ○○○○○○○○○

SOLUTION ON PAGE 179

A picnic for you and me

While the children are still busy, try and see if you can find all the differences between these two images.

DIFFICULT

I TOOK

MIN : SEC

THE DIFFERENCES I SPOTTED

07

SOLUTION ON PAGE 179

Happy divers

The word "snorkel" originates from the German word *schnorchel*, which was a tube used by German marines in World War II.

DIFFICULT

I TOOK

MIN : SEC

THE DIFFERENCES I SPOTTED

08 ○○○○○○○○

SOLUTION ON PAGE 179

To the heavens and beyond
Try and find all the differences between the two images.

DIFFICULT

I TOOK

MIN : SEC

THE DIFFERENCES I SPOTTED

SOLUTION ON PAGE 179

Her special day

Everything is perfect, except one image. Can you find it?

PHOTO FUN PICTURE PUZZLES–PEOPLE

DIFFICULT

I TOOK

MIN : SEC

SOLUTION ON PAGE 179

Punch!
Don't break into a sweat. Try and find the odd one out.

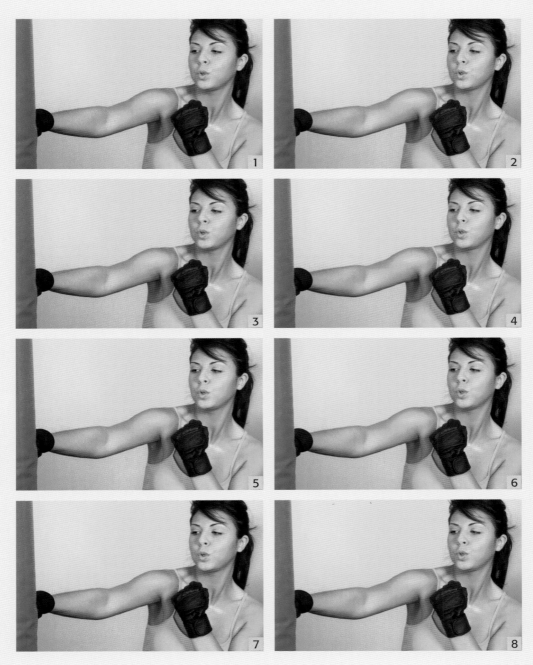

DIFFICULT

I TOOK

MIN : SEC

SOLUTION ON PAGE 179

Drum roll, please!

As the band cheers you on, try and spot all the differences between the two images.

DID YOU KNOW?
Bands of America organizes marching band competitions between high schools across the United States, the biggest being the Grand National Championships.

DIFFICULT

I TOOK

MIN : SEC

THE DIFFERENCES I SPOTTED

08 ⬍ ○○○○○○○○

SOLUTION ON PAGE 180

Hey, all!

Try and find all the differences between the two images.

DIFFICULT

I TOOK

MIN : SEC

THE DIFFERENCES I SPOTTED

06 ○○○○○○

SOLUTION ON PAGE 180

Play me a tune

Historically, it is believed that the flute originated in France about 30,000 years ago.

DIFFICULT

I TOOK

MIN : SEC

THE DIFFERENCES I SPOTTED

08 ○○○○○○○○

SOLUTION ON PAGE 180

Balancing act

In 1974 French highwalker Philippe Petit stunned the world by walking between the towers of the World Trade Center in New York City.

DIFFICULT

I TOOK

MIN : SEC

THE DIFFERENCES I SPOTTED

07

SOLUTION ON PAGE 180

We are family

"Families are like fudge—mostly sweet with a few nuts."
– Source Unknown

DIFFICULT

I TOOK

MIN : SEC

THE DIFFERENCES I SPOTTED

07 ○○○○○○○

SOLUTION ON PAGE 180

Universally treasured

"Grandma always made you feel she had been waiting to see just you all day and now the day was complete." – Marcy DeMaree

DIFFICULT

I TOOK

MIN : SEC

THE DIFFERENCES I SPOTTED

07 ⬦ ○○○○○○○

SOLUTION ON PAGE 180

Connected by smiles

Like with human beings, smiles among chimpanzees indicate happiness or pleasure. At times though, it can indicate fear.

DIFFICULT

I TOOK

MIN : SEC

THE DIFFERENCES I SPOTTED

06 ○○○○○○

SOLUTION ON PAGE 181

Friendly huddle!

Before this fun group disperses, try and locate all
the differences between the images.

DIFFICULT

I TOOK

MIN : SEC

THE DIFFERENCES I SPOTTED

07

SOLUTION ON PAGE 181

The pillars of our world

"The mark of a true professional is giving more than you get."
– Source Unknown

DIFFICULT

I TOOK

MIN : SEC

THE DIFFERENCES I SPOTTED

09 ○○○○○○○○○

SOLUTION ON PAGE 181

Skies of blue, fields of green

Can the child in you find the odd image?

DIFFICULT

I TOOK

MIN : SEC

SOLUTION ON PAGE 181

All smiles
Though the family looks perfect, there is one odd picture.
Can you find it?

DIFFICULT

I TOOK

MIN : SEC

SOLUTION ON PAGE 181

Goal!

They're ecstatic that their team just scored. See how well you do at spotting the differences between these two images.

DID YOU KNOW?
The first televised international soccer match was between England and Scotland in 1938.

DIFFICULT

I TOOK

MIN : SEC

THE DIFFERENCES I SPOTTED

 ○○○○○○

SOLUTION ON PAGE 181

Boom! Boom! Boom!

In 1641, the Modern Brazilian Carnival originated in
Rio de Janeiro.

DIFFICULT

I TOOK

MIN : SEC

THE DIFFERENCES I SPOTTED

06 ○○○○○○

SOLUTION ON PAGE 182

Friendly faces

See if you can work out where all the differences between these two images are.

DIFFICULT

I TOOK

MIN : SEC

THE DIFFERENCES I SPOTTED

08 ○○○○○○○○

SOLUTION ON PAGE 182

And the calorie count is on!

As they try and meet their target, see if you can spot all the differences between these images.

DIFFICULT

I TOOK

MIN : SEC

THE DIFFERENCES I SPOTTED

09 ○○○○○○○○○

SOLUTION ON PAGE 182

Celebrating the free spirit

"The Divine Spirit does not reside in any, except the joyful heart."
— The Talmud

DIFFICULT

I TOOK

MIN : SEC

THE DIFFERENCES I SPOTTED

06 ○○○○○○

SOLUTION ON PAGE 182

Clowning around

To trademark a clown face, the Clown and Character Registry
paints the clown's face onto a goose egg and it is archived.

DIFFICULT

I TOOK

MIN : SEC

THE DIFFERENCES I SPOTTED

07 ○○○○○○○

SOLUTION ON PAGE 182

Family fun

Universally, Children's Day is celebrated on the 20th of November.

DIFFICULT

I TOOK

MIN : SEC

THE DIFFERENCES I SPOTTED

SOLUTION ON PAGE 182

We are family

Find all the differences between the two images.

DIFFICULT

I TOOK

MIN : SEC

THE DIFFERENCES I SPOTTED

08

○○○○○○○○

SOLUTION ON PAGE 183

A ball of fun!

Even though the two images look alike, there are a few differences. Try and spot all of them.

DIFFICULT

I TOOK

MIN : SEC

THE DIFFERENCES I SPOTTED

06

SOLUTION ON PAGE 183

Girls just wanna have fun!

Get into the groove and try to spot all the differences between the two images.

DIFFICULT

I TOOK

MIN : SEC

THE DIFFERENCES I SPOTTED

06 ○○○○○○

SOLUTION ON PAGE 183

Scuba duba doo!

A natural inspiration, the Great Barrier Reef is one of the
Seven Wonders of the World.

DIFFICULT

I TOOK

MIN : SEC

THE DIFFERENCES I SPOTTED

SOLUTION ON PAGE 183

Splendor in the grass

The grand Caucasus mountain range is located in four countries:
Armenia, Azerbaijan, Georgia, and Russia.

DIFFICULT

I TOOK

MIN : SEC

THE DIFFERENCES I SPOTTED

08 ○○○○○○○○

SOLUTION ON PAGE 183

Sunny family portrait

Sit down, relax, and see if you can spot all the differences
between these two images.

DIFFICULT

I TOOK

MIN : SEC

THE DIFFERENCES I SPOTTED

08 ○○○○○○○○

SOLUTION ON PAGE 183

Nothing like your grannies to pamper you
"Nonna" in Italian, means "grandmother."

DIFFICULT

I TOOK

MIN : SEC

SOLUTION ON PAGE 184

Famous Five

The first of *The Famous Five* series, written by world-renowned author of children's books Enid Blyton, was published in 1942.

DIFFICULT

I TOOK

MIN : SEC

SOLUTION ON PAGE 184

Another pilgrimage
Pray tell me, can you spot the odd one out?

DIFFICULT

I TOOK

MIN : SEC

SOLUTION ON PAGE 184

Let's go fly a kite, up to the highest height!

Julie Andrews won an Oscar, a Golden Globe, and a British Academy Award for her role in *Mary Poppins* (1964).

DIFFICULT

I TOOK

MIN : SEC

SOLUTION ON PAGE 184

Cheers!

Before they order the next round, can you spot all the differences between these two images?

DID YOU KNOW?

In the 1790s, "happy hour" began at three o'clock in the afternoon and cocktails continued until dinner, at which only wine would be served.

COMPLEX

I TOOK

MIN : SEC

THE DIFFERENCES I SPOTTED

09 ○○○○○○○○○

SOLUTION ON PAGE 184

Let's celebrate!
As this happy family celebrates the joys of life, try and spot the differences between these two images.

COMPLEX

I TOOK

MIN : SEC

THE DIFFERENCES I SPOTTED

09 ○○○○○○○○○

SOLUTION ON PAGE 184

Mapping the future

"An economist is an expert who will know tomorrow why the things he predicted yesterday didn't happen today." – Laurence J. Peter

COMPLEX

I TOOK

MIN : SEC

THE DIFFERENCES I SPOTTED

08 ○○○○○○○○

SOLUTION ON PAGE 185

Engineering for tomorrow

See if you can find a way to spot all the differences between these images.

COMPLEX

I TOOK

MIN : SEC

THE DIFFERENCES I SPOTTED

07 ○○○○○○○

SOLUTION ON PAGE 185

Make or break moments

Before the deal is closed, can you spot all the differences between the two images?

THE DIFFERENCES I SPOTTED

SOLUTION ON PAGE 185

Huddle up!

Walter Camp, popularly known as the Father of American Football, formed the rules of the sport.

COMPLEX

I TOOK

MIN : SEC

THE DIFFERENCES I SPOTTED

07 ○○○○○○○

SOLUTION ON PAGE 185

Racing for health

Time is racing by! See how quickly you can find all the differences between the two images?

COMPLEX

I TOOK

MIN : SEC

THE DIFFERENCES I SPOTTED

05 ○○○○○

SOLUTION ON PAGE 185

If looks could kill

In the 1970s, Abraham and Strauss, a mega department store based in New York City, made mannequin-modeling popular.

COMPLEX

I TOOK

MIN : SEC

SOLUTION ON PAGE 185

Mind over matter
All the mess is distracting, so they tried to clean up.
Can you spot the difference?

COMPLEX

I TOOK

MIN : SEC

SOLUTION ON PAGE 186

Step up! Shape up!

Give your mind a mental workout, by locating the odd one out.

COMPLEX

I TOOK

MIN : SEC

SOLUTION ON PAGE 186

The loser pays for lunch

Before the race concludes, can you spot the odd one out?

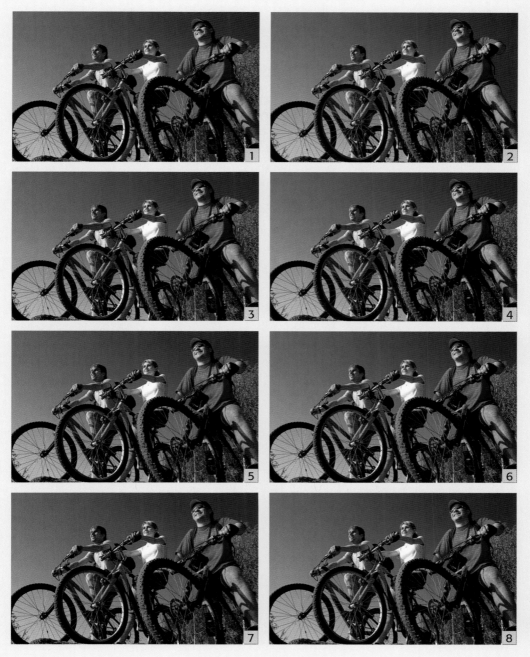

COMPLEX

I TOOK

MIN : SEC

SOLUTION ON PAGE 186

Eat up!

As they enjoy this sushi, see if you can spot all the differences between these two images.

DID YOU KNOW?

Traditionally, the Japanese do not have sake with sushi as it is believed that since they are both rice based, they do not complement one another.

COMPLEX

I TOOK

MIN : SEC

THE DIFFERENCES I SPOTTED

08 ○○○○○○○○

SOLUTION ON PAGE 186

We'll shop but never drop
These girls are on the quest to find the perfect dress.
Can you find the differences between the two images?

COMPLEX

I TOOK

MIN : SEC

THE DIFFERENCES I SPOTTED

06 ○○○○○○

SOLUTION ON PAGE 186

Nothing less than perfection will do

Work up an appetite by attempting to find all the differences between the two images.

COMPLEX

I TOOK

MIN : SEC

THE DIFFERENCES I SPOTTED

10 ○○○○○○○○○○

SOLUTION ON PAGE 186

Wonders never cease

Statins, also known as the "drug of the decade," lowers cholesterol, reducing the chances of heart attacks and strokes.

COMPLEX

I TOOK

MIN : SEC

THE DIFFERENCES I SPOTTED

06 ○○○○○○

SOLUTION ON PAGE 187

Rock on!
As they pump out the beats, do you think you can find all the differences between the two images?

COMPLEX

I TOOK

MIN : SEC

THE DIFFERENCES I SPOTTED

08 ○○○○○○○○

SOLUTION ON PAGE 187

Live for today, plan for tomorrow, party tonight!

Before you go partying all night, try and find the differences between the two images.

COMPLEX

I TOOK

MIN : SEC

THE DIFFERENCES I SPOTTED

06 ○○○○○○

SOLUTION ON PAGE 187

The game just got even more interesting

See how well you score against the clock. Try and find all the differences between the two images as quickly as possible.

COMPLEX

I TOOK

MIN : SEC

THE DIFFERENCES I SPOTTED

06 ○○○○○○

SOLUTION ON PAGE 187

The hidden picture revealed
"Poverty is the worst form of violence." — Mahatma Gandhi

COMPLEX

I TOOK

MIN : SEC

THE DIFFERENCES I SPOTTED

08 ○○○○○○○○

SOLUTION ON PAGE 187

A fortress of leaders

"In the business world, everyone is paid in two coins: cash and experience. Take the experience first; the cash will come later."
– Henry Ford

COMPLEX

I TOOK

MIN : SEC

THE DIFFERENCES I SPOTTED

SOLUTION ON PAGE 187

Save the last dance for me
Before the sun sets, spot the odd image.

COMPLEX

I TOOK

MIN : SEC

SOLUTION ON PAGE 188

Say cheese!

Picture perfect, but one. Can you locate it?

COMPLEX

I TOOK

MIN : SEC

SOLUTION ON PAGE 188

The heat is on

The odd image is lost in the Kalahari Desert. Can you find it?

COMPLEX

I TOOK

MIN : SEC

SOLUTION ON PAGE 188

Say a little prayer for me
Can you spot the odd image?

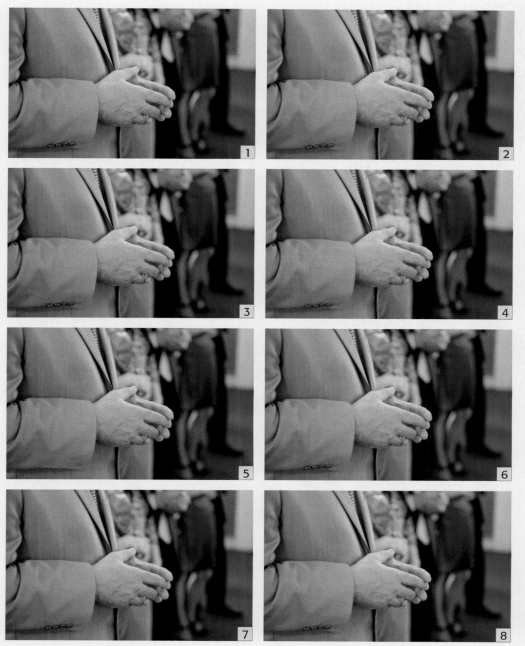

COMPLEX

I TOOK

MIN : SEC

SOLUTION ON PAGE 188

The different faces of the corporate world

"You can't just ask customers what they want and then try and give it to them. By the time you get it built, they'll want something new." – Steve Jobs

DID YOU KNOW?
Historically, it is believed that the first multinational company was the East India Company.

COMPLEX

I TOOK

MIN : SEC

THE DIFFERENCES I SPOTTED

10 ○○○○○○○○○○

SOLUTION ON PAGE 188

My station

The London Underground began in 1863, and, despite its name, more than half the network is above the ground.

COMPLEX

I TOOK

MIN : SEC

THE DIFFERENCES I SPOTTED

08 ○○○○○○○○

SOLUTION ON PAGE 188

Luau mania

A *luau* is a Hawaiian feast where people eat, drink, dance, and make merry. Keeping that spirit in mind, enjoy solving this fun puzzle.

COMPLEX

I TOOK

MIN : SEC

THE DIFFERENCES I SPOTTED

SOLUTION ON PAGE 189

Santa Claus is coming to town

A mixture of secular and religious traditions, Christmas is a holiday celebrated by people from all around the world.

COMPLEX

I TOOK

MIN : SEC

THE DIFFERENCES I SPOTTED

07

SOLUTION ON PAGE 189

And a one, two, one, two, three

As they complete their workout, see if you can work out where all the differences between these two images are.

COMPLEX

I TOOK

MIN : SEC

THE DIFFERENCES I SPOTTED

05 ○○○○○

SOLUTION ON PAGE 189

I'm going to dance all night

Donna Summer, a performer from the 1970's was one of the pioneers of disco and held the title "the queen of disco."

COMPLEX

I TOOK

MIN : SEC

THE DIFFERENCES I SPOTTED

08 ○○○○○○○○

SOLUTION ON PAGE 189

Serenading you

An orchestra has four kinds of stringed instruments: cellos, double basses, violas, and violins.

COMPLEX

I TOOK

MIN : SEC

THE DIFFERENCES I SPOTTED

07 ○○○○○○○

SOLUTION ON PAGE 189

Let me show you something
Can you spot all the differences between the two images?

COMPLEX

I TOOK

MIN : SEC

THE DIFFERENCES I SPOTTED

09 ○○○○○○○○○

SOLUTION ON PAGE 189

Party on!

As this band of girls paints the town red, try and find all the differences between the two images.

COMPLEX

I TOOK

MIN : SEC

THE DIFFERENCES I SPOTTED

07 ○○○○○○○

SOLUTION ON PAGE 190

Jet-setting genius

Before the flight arrives at its destination, try and locate all the differences between the two images.

COMPLEX

I TOOK

MIN : SEC

THE DIFFERENCES I SPOTTED

SOLUTION ON PAGE 190

One block at a time

Try and see if you can find all the differences between these two images.

COMPLEX

I TOOK

MIN : SEC

THE DIFFERENCES I SPOTTED

08 ○○○○○○○○

SOLUTION ON PAGE 190

Blurry

We know it's getting harder to see, but give it your best shot and find all the differences between the two images.

COMPLEX

THE DIFFERENCES I SPOTTED

07

SOLUTION ON PAGE 190

Happy Birthday to you

Even though it may not be your birthday today, have some fun by finding the differences between these images.

COMPLEX

I TOOK

MIN : SEC

THE DIFFERENCES I SPOTTED

08 ⟩ ○○○○○○○○

SOLUTION ON PAGE 190

A concert for inspiration

Try and beat the clock by spotting all the differences between these images as quickly as you can.

COMPLEX

I TOOK

MIN : SEC

THE DIFFERENCES I SPOTTED

 ○○○○○○○

SOLUTION ON PAGE 190

Flowery canopy

Add to the pleasure of solving this puzzle by stepping outdoors and enjoying the gifts of nature.

COMPLEX

I TOOK

MIN : SEC

THE DIFFERENCES I SPOTTED

08

SOLUTION ON PAGE 191

Time is money
"Bizjet" is the colloquial term for a business jet or private jet.

COMPLEX

I TOOK

MIN : SEC

THE DIFFERENCES I SPOTTED

06 ○○○○○○

SOLUTION ON PAGE 191

Thumbs up!

The gesture that in the West popularly denotes "well done" is considered an obscene gesture in Iran, Bangladesh, and Iran.

COMPLEX

I TOOK

MIN : SEC

THE DIFFERENCES I SPOTTED

SOLUTION ON PAGE 191

Rat race

"You don't have to be great to start, but you have to start to be great." – Zig Ziglar

COMPLEX

I TOOK

MIN : SEC

SOLUTION ON PAGE 191

Play the right note!
Before she stops playing, can you find the odd one out?

COMPLEX

I TOOK

MIN : SEC

SOLUTION ON PAGE 191

Wearing a mask is the most liberating feeling

Most Halloween masks are orange and black because orange symbolizes the fall season and black, death.

COMPLEX

I TOOK

MIN : SEC

SOLUTION ON PAGE 191

Dinner time!

Everything is perfect but one image. Can you spot it?

COMPLEX

I TOOK

MIN : SEC

SOLUTION ON PAGE 192

Page 09:

Page 10:

Page 11:

Page 12:

Page 13:

Page 14:

Page 15:

Page 16:

Page 17:

Page 18:

Page 19:

Page 20:

Page 21:

Page 23:

Page 24:

Page 25:

Page 26:

Page 27:

Page 28:

Page 29:

Page 30:

Page 31:

Page 32:

Page 33:

Page 34:

Page 35:

Page 37:

Page 38:

Page 39:

Page 40:

Page 41:

Page 42:

Page 43:

Page 44:

Page 45:

Page 46:

Page 47:

Page 49:

Page 50:

Page 51:

Page 52:

Page 53:

Page 54:

Page 55:

Page 56:

Page 57:

Page 58:

Page 59:

Page 60:

Page 61:

Page 65:

Page 66:

Page 67:

Page 68:

Page 69:

Page 70:

Page 71:

Page 72:

Page 73:

Page 74:

Page 75:

Page 77:

Page 78:

Page 79:

Page 80:

Page 81:

Page 82:

Page 83:

Page 84:

Page 85:

Page 86:

Page 87:

Page 89:

Page 90:

Page 91:

Page 92:

Page 93:

Page 94:

Page 95:

Page 96:

Page 97:

Page 98:

Page 99:

Page 101:

Page 102:

Page 103:

Page 104:

Page 105:

Page 106:

Page 107:

Page 108:

Page 109:

Page 110:

Page 111:

Page 112:

Page 113:

Page 114:

Page 115:

Page 116:

Page 117:

Page 121:

Page 122:

Page 123:

Page 124:

Page 125:

Page 126:

Page 127:

Page 128:

Page 129:

Page 130:

Page 131:

Page 133:

Page 134:

Page 135:

Page 136:

Page 137:

Page 138:

Page 139:

Page 140:

Page 141:

Page 142:

Page 143:

Page 144:

Page 145:

Page 147:

Page 148:

Page 149:

Page 150:

Page 151:

Page 152:

Page 153:

Page 154:

Page 155:

Page 156:

Page 157:

Page 158:

Page 159:

Page 160:

Page 161:

Page 162:

Page 163:

Page 164:

Page 165:

Page 166:

Page 167: